Lent
with Benedict XVI

Season of new life

*All booklets are published thanks to the
generous support of the members of the
Catholic Truth Society*

CATHOLIC TRUTH SOCIETY
PUBLISHERS TO THE HOLY SEE

Contents

Rediscovering our Baptism

"You were buried with him in baptism,
in which you were also raised with him."
(cf. *Col* 2:12)

The Lenten period, which leads us to the celebration of Holy Easter, is for the Church a most valuable and important liturgical time, in view of which I am pleased to offer a specific word in order that it may be lived with due diligence. As she awaits the definitive encounter with her Spouse in the eternal Easter, the Church community, assiduous in prayer and charitable works, intensifies her journey in purifying the spirit, so as to draw more abundantly from the Mystery of Redemption the new life in Christ the Lord (cf. *Preface I of Lent*).

Baptism permits us to reach the stature of Christ

This very life was already bestowed upon us on the day of our Baptism, when we "become sharers in Christ's death and Resurrection", and there began for us "the joyful and exulting adventure of his disciples" *(Homily on the Feast of the Baptism of the Lord*, 10 January, 2010). In his Letters, St Paul repeatedly insists on the singular communion with the Son of God that this washing brings about. The fact that, in most cases, Baptism is received in infancy highlights how it is a gift of God: no one earns eternal life through their own efforts. The mercy of God, which cancels sin and, at the same time, allows us to experience in our lives "the mind of Christ Jesus" (*Phil* 2:5), is given to men and women freely. The Apostle to the Gentiles, in the *Letter to the Philippians*, expresses the meaning of the transformation that takes place through participation in the death and resurrection of Christ, pointing to its goal: that "I may come to know him and the power of his resurrection, and partake of his sufferings by being molded to the pattern of his death, striving towards the goal of resurrection from the dead" (*Phil* 3:10-11). Hence, Baptism is not a rite from the past, but the encounter with Christ, which informs the entire existence of the baptized, imparting divine life and calling for sincere conversion; initiated and supported by Grace, it permits the baptized to reach the adult stature of Christ.

Experiencing saving grace

A *particular connection* binds Baptism to Lent as the favorable time to experience this saving Grace. The Fathers of the Second Vatican Council exhorted all of the Church's Pastors to make greater use "of the baptismal features proper to the Lenten liturgy" (Constitution on the Sacred Liturgy *Sacrosanctum concilium*, n. 109). In fact, the Church has always associated the Easter Vigil with the celebration of Baptism: this Sacrament realizes the great mystery in which man dies to sin, is made a sharer in the new life of the Risen Christ and receives the same Spirit of God who raised Jesus from the dead (cf. *Rm* 8:11). This free gift must always be rekindled in each one of us, and Lent offers us a path like that of the catechumenate, which, for the Christians of the early Church, just as for catechumens today, is an irreplaceable school of faith and Christian life. Truly, they live their Baptism as an act that shapes their entire existence.

Guided by the word of God

In order to undertake more seriously our journey towards Easter and prepare ourselves to celebrate the Resurrection of the Lord – the most joyous and solemn feast of the entire liturgical year – what could be more appropriate than allowing ourselves to be guided by the Word of God? For this reason, the Church, in the Gospel texts of the Sundays of Lent, leads us to a particularly intense encounter with the Lord, calling us to retrace the steps of Christian initiation: for catechumens, in preparation for receiving the Sacrament of rebirth; for the baptized, in light of the new and decisive steps to be taken in the *sequela Christi* and a fuller giving of oneself to him.

Our condition as human beings

The First Sunday of the Lenten journey reveals our condition as human beings here on earth. The victorious battle against temptation, the starting point of Jesus' mission, is an invitation to become aware of our own fragility in order to accept the Grace that frees from sin and infuses new strength in Christ – the way, the truth and the life (cf. *Ordo Initiationis Christianae Adultorum*, n. 25). It is a powerful reminder that Christian faith implies, following the example of Jesus and in union with him, a battle "against the ruling forces who are masters of the darkness in this world" (*Eph* 6:12), in which the devil is at work and never tires – even today – of tempting whoever wishes to draw close to the Lord: Christ emerges victorious to open also our hearts to hope and guide us in overcoming the seductions of evil.

The glory of Christ

The Gospel of the Transfiguration of the Lord puts before our eyes the glory of Christ, which anticipates the resurrection and announces the divinization of man. The Christian community becomes aware that Jesus leads it, like the Apostles Peter, James and John "up a high mountain by themselves" (*Mt* 17:1), to receive once again in Christ, as sons and daughters in the Son, the gift of the Grace of God: "This is my Son, the Beloved; he enjoys my favor. Listen to him" (*Mt* 17:5). It is the invitation to take a distance from the noisiness of everyday life in order to immerse oneself in God's presence. He desires to hand down to us, each day, a Word that penetrates the depths of our spirit, where we discern good from evil (cf. *Heb* 4:12), reinforcing our will to follow the Lord.

Our thirst for goodness, truth and beauty

The question that Jesus puts to the Samaritan woman: "Give me a drink" (*Jn* 4:7), is presented to us in the liturgy of the third Sunday; it expresses the passion of God for every man and woman, and wishes to awaken in our hearts the desire for the gift of "a spring of water within, welling up for eternal life" (*Jn* 4:14): this is the gift of the Holy Spirit, who transforms Christians into "true worshipers," capable of praying to the Father "in spirit and truth" (*Jn* 4:23). Only this water can extinguish our thirst for goodness, truth and beauty! Only this water, given to us by the Son, can irrigate the deserts of our restless and unsatisfied soul, until it "finds rest in God", as per the famous words of St Augustine.

Children of the light

The Sunday of the man born blind presents Christ as the light of the world. The Gospel confronts each one of us with the question: "Do you believe in the Son of man?" "Lord, I believe!" (*Jn* 9:35. 38), the man born blind joyfully exclaims, giving voice to all believers. The miracle of this healing is a sign that Christ wants not only to give us sight, but also open our interior vision, so that our faith may become ever deeper and we may recognize him as our only Savior. He illuminates all that is dark in life and leads men and women to live as "children of the light".

The ultimate mystery of our existence

On the fifth Sunday, when the resurrection of Lazarus is proclaimed, we are faced with the ultimate mystery of our existence: "I am the resurrection and the life... Do you believe this?" (*Jn* 11:25-26). For the Christian community, it is the moment to place with sincerity – together with Martha – all of our hopes in Jesus of Nazareth: "Yes, Lord, I believe that you are the Christ, the Son of God, the one who was to come into this world" (*Jn* 11:27). Communion with Christ in this life prepares us to overcome the barrier of death, so that we may live eternally with him. Faith in the resurrection of the dead and hope in eternal life open our eyes to the ultimate meaning of our existence: God created men and women for resurrection and life, and this truth gives an authentic and definitive meaning to human history, to the personal and social lives of men and women, to culture, politics and the economy. Without the light of faith, the entire universe finishes shut within a tomb devoid of any future, any hope.

The Lenten journey finds its fulfillment in the Paschal Triduum, especially in the Great Vigil of the Holy Night: renewing our baptismal promises, we reaffirm that Christ is the Lord of our life, that life which God bestowed upon us when we were reborn of "water and Holy Spirit", and we profess again our firm commitment to respond to the action of the Grace in order to be his disciples.

Love in its most extreme form

By immersing ourselves into the death and resurrection of Christ through the Sacrament of Baptism, we are moved to free our hearts every day from the burden of material things, from a self-centered relationship with the "world" that impoverishes us and prevents us from being available and open to God and our neighbor. In Christ, God revealed himself as Love (cf. 1 *Jn* 4:7-10). The Cross of Christ, the "word of the Cross", manifests God's saving power (cf. 1 *Cor* 1:18), that is given to raise men and women anew and bring them salvation: it is love in its most extreme form (cf. Encyclical *Deus caritas est*, n. 12).

Fasting opens us to God and others

Through the traditional practices of fasting, almsgiving and prayer, which are an expression of our commitment to conversion, Lent teaches us how to live the love of Christ in an ever more radical way. *Fasting,* which can have various motivations, takes on a profoundly religious significance for the Christian: by rendering our table poorer, we learn to overcome selfishness in order to live in the logic of gift and love; by bearing some form of deprivation – and not just what is in excess – we learn to look away from our "ego", to discover Someone close to us and to recognize God in the face of so many brothers and sisters. For Christians, fasting, far from being depressing, opens us ever more to God and to the needs of others, thus allowing love of God to become also love of our neighbor (cf. *Mk* 12:31).

Almsgiving – the capacity to share

In our journey, we are often faced with the temptation of accumulating and love of money that undermine God's primacy in our lives. The greed of possession leads to violence, exploitation and death; for this, the Church, especially during the Lenten period, reminds us to practice *almsgiving* – which is the capacity to share. The idolatry of goods, on the other hand, not only causes us to drift away from others, but divests man, making him unhappy, deceiving him, deluding him without fulfilling its promises, since it puts materialistic goods in the place of God, the only source of life. How can we understand God's paternal goodness, if our heart is full of egoism and our own projects, deceiving us that our future is guaranteed? The temptation is to think, just like the rich man in the parable: "My soul, you have plenty of good things laid by for many years to come…". We are all aware of the Lord's judgment: "Fool! This very night the demand will be made for your soul…" (*Lk* 12:19-20). The practice of almsgiving is a reminder of God's primacy and turns our attention towards others, so that we may rediscover how good our Father is, and receive his mercy.

An irreplaceable form of prayer

During the entire Lenten period, the Church offers us God's Word with particular abundance. By meditating and internalizing the Word in order to live it every day, we learn a precious and irreplaceable form of prayer; by attentively listening to God, who continues to speak to our hearts, we nourish the itinerary of faith initiated on the day of our Baptism. Prayer also allows us to gain a new concept of time: without the perspective of eternity and transcendence, in fact, time simply directs our steps towards a horizon without a future. Instead, when we pray, we find time for God, to understand that his "words will not pass away" (cf. *Mk* 13:31), to enter into that intimate communion with Him "that no one shall take from you" (*Jn* 16:22), opening us to the hope that does not disappoint, eternal life.

A deep conversion

In synthesis, the Lenten journey, in which we are invited to contemplate the Mystery of the Cross, is meant to reproduce within us "the pattern of his death" (*Ph* 3:10), so as to effect a deep *conversion* in our lives; that we may be transformed by the action of the Holy Spirit, like St Paul on the road to Damascus; that we may firmly orient our existence according to the will of God; that we may be freed of our egoism, overcoming the instinct to dominate others and opening us to the love of Christ. The Lenten period is a favorable time to recognize our weakness and to accept, through a sincere inventory of our life, the renewing Grace of the Sacrament of Penance, and walk resolutely towards Christ.

Through the personal encounter with our Redeemer and through fasting, almsgiving and prayer, the journey of conversion towards Easter leads us to rediscover our Baptism. This Lent, let us renew our acceptance of the Grace that God bestowed upon us at that moment, so that it may illuminate and guide all of our actions. What the Sacrament signifies and realizes, we are called to experience every day by following Christ in an ever more generous and authentic manner. In this our itinerary, let us entrust ourselves to the Virgin Mary, who generated the Word of God in faith and in the flesh, so that we may immerse ourselves – just as she did – in the death and resurrection of her Son Jesus, and possess eternal life.

Strengthen our desire to change – Ash Wednesday

On this day, marked by the austere symbol of ashes, we enter the Season of Lent, beginning a spiritual journey that prepares us for celebrating worthily the Easter Mysteries. The blessed ashes imposed upon our forehead are a sign that reminds us of our condition as creatures, that invites us to repent, and to intensify our commitment to convert, to follow the Lord ever more closely.

Lent is a journey, it means accompanying Jesus who goes up to Jerusalem, the place of the fulfilment of his mystery of Passion, death and Resurrection; it reminds us that Christian life is a "way" to take, not so much consistent with a law to observe as with the very Person of Christ, to encounter, to welcome, to follow.

Take up your cross

Indeed, Jesus says to us: "If any man would come after me, let him deny himself and take up his cross daily and follow me" (*Lk* 9:23). In other words he tells us that in order to attain, with him, the light and joy of the Resurrection, the victory of life, of love and of goodness, we too must take up our daily cross, as a beautiful passage from the *Imitation of Christ* urges us: "Take up your cross, therefore, and follow Jesus, and you shall enter eternal life. He himself opened the way before you in carrying his Cross (*Jn* 19:17), and upon it he died for you, that you too, might take up your cross and long to die upon it. If you die with him, you shall also live with him, and if you share his suffering, you shall also share his glory" (Book 2, chapter 12, n. 2).

Convert our hearts

In Holy Mass of the First Sunday of Lent we shall pray: "Father, through our observance of Lent, sign of the sacrament of our conversion, help us to understand the meaning of your Son's death and Resurrection, and teach us to reflect it in our lives" *(Opening Prayer)*.

This is an invocation that we address to God because we know that he alone can convert our hearts. And it is above all in the Liturgy, by participating in the holy mysteries, that we are led to make this journey with the Lord; it means learning at the school of Jesus, reviewing the events that brought salvation to us but not as a mere commemoration, a remembrance of past events. In the liturgical actions Christ makes himself present through the power of the Holy Spirit and these saving events become real.

Today is a favourable time

There is a keyword that recurs frequently in the Liturgy to indicate this: the word "today"; and it should be understood in its original and practical, rather than metaphorical, sense. *Today* God reveals his law and we are granted to choose *today* between good and evil, between life and death (*cf. Dt* 30:19). *Today* "the Kingdom of God is at hand; repent and believe in the Gospel" (*Mk* 1:15). *Today* Christ died on Calvary and rose from the dead; he ascended into Heaven and is seated at the right hand of the Father; *today* the Holy Spirit is given to us; *today* is a favourable time.

A baptismal journey

Taking part in the Liturgy thus means immersing our life in the mystery of Christ, in his enduring presence so as to follow a path on which we enter his death and Resurrection in order to have life. The Sundays of Lent, in this liturgical year of Cycle A in a quite particular way, introduce us to the experience of a baptismal journey, almost as if we were retracing the path of the catechumens, of those who are preparing to receive Baptism, in order to rekindle this gift within us and to ensure that our life may recover a sense of the demands and commitments of this sacrament which is at the root of our Christian life.

In the Message for this Lent I wished to recall the particular connection that binds Baptism to the Season of Lent. The Church has always associated the Easter Vigil with the celebration of Baptism, step by step. In it is brought about that great mystery through which man, dead to sin, is enabled to share in new life in the Risen Christ and receives the Spirit of God who raised Jesus from the dead (*cf. Rom* 8:11).

The Readings we shall listen to on the coming Sundays and to which I ask you to pay special attention are taken up precisely by the ancient tradition which accompanied catechumens in the discovery of Baptism. These Readings are the great proclamation of what God brings about in this sacrament, a wonderful baptismal catechesis addressed to each one of us.

Courage to face the struggle

The First Sunday of Lent, known as the "Sunday of the Temptation" because it presents Jesus' temptations in the wilderness, invites us to renew our definitive adherence to God and, in order to remain faithful to him, to face courageously the struggle that awaits us.

Over and over again we need determination, resistance to evil, we need to follow Jesus. On this Sunday, after hearing the testimony of the godparents and catechists, the Church celebrates the election of those who are admitted to the Easter sacraments.

Faith and divine sonship

The Second Sunday is called "of Abraham and of the Transfiguration". Baptism is the sacrament of faith and of divine sonship; like Abraham, Father of believers, we too are asked to set out, to depart from our land, to give up the security we have created for ourselves in order to place our trust in God; the destination is glimpsed in the Transfiguration of Christ, the beloved Son, in whom we too become "sons of God".

The water that saves

On the following Sundays, Baptism is presented in images of water, light and life. The Third Sunday makes us meet the Samaritan woman (*cf. Jn* 4:5-42). Like Israel in the Exodus, in Baptism we too have received the water that saves; Jesus, as the Samaritan woman says, has living water that quenches all thirst; and this water is the Spirit himself. On this Sunday the Church celebrates the First Scrutiny of the catechumens and during the week presents to them the Creed: the profession of faith.

Children of light

The Fourth Sunday makes us reflect on the experience of the "man blind from birth" (*cf. Jn* 9:1-41). In Baptism, we are set free from the shadow of evil and receive Christ's light in order to live as children of light. We too must learn to see in Christ's Face God's presence, hence light.

The Second Scrutiny on the catechumen's journey is celebrated.

Passing from death to life

Lastly, the Fifth Sunday presents to us the raising of Lazarus (*cf. Jn* 11:1-45). In Baptism we passed from death to life and were enabled to please God, to make the former person die so as to live by the Spirit of the Risen One. The Third Scrutiny for the catechumens is celebrated and during the week the *Lord's Prayer* is presented to them.

The full reality of fasting

In the Church's tradition, this journey we are asked to take in Lent is marked by certain practices: fasting, almsgiving and prayer. Fasting means abstinence from food but includes other forms of privation for a more modest life. However, all this is not yet the full reality of fasting: it is an outer sign of an inner reality, of our commitment, with God's help, to abstain from evil and to live by the Gospel. Those who are unable to nourish themselves with the word of God do not fast properly.

Fasting linked to almsgiving

In the Christian tradition fasting is closely linked to almsgiving. St Leo the Great taught in one of his Discourses on Lent: "All that each Christian is bound to do in every season he must now do with greater solicitude and devotion in order to fulfil the apostolic prescription of Lenten fasting consistently, not only in abstinence from food but also and above all from sin. Furthermore, with this holy fasting which is only right, no work may be more fruitfully associated than almsgiving which, under the one name of 'mercy', embraces many good works. The field of works of mercy is immense. It is not only the rich and the well-off who can benefit others with almsgiving, but also those of modest means and even the poor. Thus, although their futures differ, all may be the same in the soul's sentiments of piety" (*Sermon* VI *on Lent*, 2: PL 54, 286).

The two wings of prayer

St Gregory the Great recalled in his *Pastoral Rule* that fasting is sanctified by the virtues that go with it, especially by charity, by every act of generosity, giving to the poor and needy the equivalent of something we ourselves have given up (*cf.* 19, 10-11). Lent, moreover, is a privileged period for prayer. St Augustine said that fasting and almsgiving are "the two wings of prayer" which enable it to gain momentum and more easily reach even to God.

He said: "In this way our prayers, made in humility and charity, in fasting and almsgiving, in temperance and in the forgiveness of offences, giving good things and not returning those that are bad, keeping away from evil and doing good, seek peace and achieve it. On the wings of these virtues our prayers fly safely and are more easily carried to Heaven, where Christ our Peace has preceded us" (*Sermon* 206, 3 *on Lent:* PL 38, 1042).

Put prayer above all things

The Church knows that because of our weakness it is difficult to create silence in order to come before God and to acquire an awareness of our condition as creatures who depend on him, as sinners in need of his love. It is for this reason that in Lent she asks us to pray more faithfully, more intensely, and to prolong our meditation on the word of God.

St John Chrysostom urged: "Embellish your house with modesty and humility with the practice of prayer. Make your dwelling place shine with the light of justice; adorn its walls with good works, like a lustre of pure gold, and replace walls and precious stones with faith and supernatural magnanimity, putting prayer above all other things, high up in the gables, to give the whole complex decorum.

"You will thus prepare a worthy dwelling place for the Lord, you will welcome him in a splendid palace. He will grant you to transform your soul into a temple of his presence" (*Homily 6 on Prayer:* PG 64, 466).

Follow Christ more consistently

On this Lenten journey let us be careful to accept Christ's invitation to follow him more decisively and consistently, renewing the grace and commitments of our Baptism, to cast off the former person within us and put on Christ, in order to arrive at Easter renewed and able to say, with St Paul: "It is no longer I who live, but Christ who lives in me" (*Gal* 2:20). I wish you all a good Lenten journey!

Authentic conversion to God

We wish to commit ourselves to converting our hearts to the horizons of Grace. People generally associate this Season with the sadness and dreariness of life. On the contrary, it is a precious gift of God, a strong time full of meaning on the Church's path, it is the journey that leads to the Passover of the Lord.

The biblical Readings of today's celebration give us instructions for living this spiritual experience to the full. "Return to me with all your heart" (*Joel* 2:12). In the First Reading from the Book of the Prophet Joel we heard these words with which God invites the Jewish people to sincere and unostentatious repentance. This is not a superficial and transitory conversion; but a spiritual itinerary that deeply concerns the attitude of the conscience and implies sincere determination to reform.

The Prophet draws inspiration from the plague of locusts that descended on the people, destroying their crops, to ask them for inner repentance and to rend their hearts rather than their clothing (*cf.* 2:13).

In other words, it is in practice a question of adopting an attitude of authentic conversion to God — of returning to him — recognizing his holiness, his power, his majesty.

His is a regenerating mercy

And this conversion is possible because God is rich in mercy and great in love. His is a regenerating mercy that creates within us a pure heart, renews in our depths a firm spirit, restoring the joy of salvation (*cf. Ps* 51 [50]:14). God, in fact — as the Prophet says — does not want the sinner to die but to convert and live (*cf. Ezek* 33:11).

The creation of a favourable penitential environment

The Prophet Joel orders in the Lord's name the creation of a favourable penitential environment: the trumpet must be blown to convoke the gathering and reawaken consciences. The Lenten Season proposes to us this liturgical and penitential environment: a journey of 40 days in which to experience God's merciful love effectively.

Return to me with all your heart

Today the appeal: "Return to me with all your heart", resounds for us. Today it is we who are called to convert our hearts to God, in the constant awareness that we cannot achieve conversion on our own, with our own efforts, because it is God who converts us. Furthermore, he offers us his forgiveness, asking us to return to him, to give us a new heart cleansed of the evil that clogs it, to enable us to share in his joy. Our world needs to be converted by God, it needs his forgiveness, his love, it needs a new heart.

Be reconciled to God

"Be reconciled to God" (2 *Cor* 5:20). In the Second Reading St Paul offers us another element on our journey of conversion. The Apostle invites us to remove our gaze from him and to pay attention instead to the One who sent him and to the content of the message he bears: "So we are ambassadors for Christ, God making his appeal through us. We therefore beseech you on behalf of Christ, be reconciled to God" (*ibid.*).

An ambassador repeats what he has heard his Lord say and speaks with the authority and within the limits that he has been given. Anyone who serves in the office of ambassador must not draw attention to himself but must put himself at the service of the message to be transmitted and of the one who has sent it.

This is how St Paul acted in exercising his ministry as a preacher of the word of God and an Apostle of Jesus Christ. He does not shrink from the duty he has received, but carries it out with total dedication, asking us to open ourselves to Grace, to let God convert us. He writes: "Working together with him, then, we entreat you not to accept the grace of God in vain" (2 *Cor* 6:1).

Christ's call to conversion – the path of penance and renewal

"Christ's call to conversion", the *Catechism of the Catholic Church* tells us, "continues to resound in the lives of Christians... [it] is an uninterrupted task for the whole Church" which, "clasping sinners to her bosom", and "'at once holy and always in need of purification... follows constantly the path of penance and renewal". "This endeavour of conversion is not just a human work. It is the movement of a 'contrite heart' (*Ps* 51:17), drawn and moved by grace to respond to the merciful love of God who loved us first" (n. 1428).

St Paul was speaking to the Christians of Corinth but through them he intended to address all people. Indeed, all people have always needed God's grace which illuminates minds and hearts. And the Apostle immediately insists "Behold, now is the acceptable time; behold, now is the day of salvation" (2 *Cor* 6:2). All can open themselves to God's action, to his love; with our evangelical witness we Christians must be a living message; indeed in many cases we are the only Gospel that men and women of today still read.

This is our responsibility, following in St Paul's footsteps, a further reason for living Lent fully: in order to bear a witness of faith lived to a world in difficulty in need of returning to God, in need of conversion.

Watch out for signs of superiority and self–love

"Beware of practising your piety before men in order to be seen by them" (*Mt* 6:1). In today's Gospel Jesus reinterprets the three fundamental pious practices prescribed by Mosaic law. Almsgiving, prayer and fasting characterize the Jew who observes the law. In the course of time these prescriptions were corroded by the rust of external formalism or even transformed into a sign of superiority.

In these three practices Jesus highlights a common temptation. Doing a good deed almost instinctively gives rise to the desire to be esteemed and admired for the good action, in other words to gain a reward. And on the one hand this closes us in on ourselves and on the other, it brings us out of ourselves because we live oriented to what others think of us or admire in us.

In proposing these prescriptions anew the Lord Jesus does not ask for formal respect of a law that is alien to the human being, imposed by a severe legislator as a heavy burden, but invites us to rediscover these three pious practices by living them more deeply, not out of self-love but out of love of God, as a means on the journey of conversion to him. Alms-giving, prayer and fasting: these are the path of the divine pedagogy that accompanies us not only in Lent, towards the encounter with the Risen Lord; a course to take without ostentation, in the certainty that the heavenly Father can read and also see into our heart in secret.

A more generous practice of mortification

Let us set out confidently and joyfully on the Lenten journey. Forty days separate us from Easter; this "strong" season of the liturgical year is a favourable time which is granted to us so that we may attend more closely to our conversion, listen more intensely to the word of God and intensify our prayer and penance. We thereby open our hearts to docile acceptance of the divine will for a more generous practice of mortification thanks to which we can go more generously to the aid of our needy neighbour: a spiritual journey that prepares us to relive the Paschal Mystery.

May Mary, our guide on the Lenten journey, lead us to ever deeper knowledge of the dead and Risen Christ, help us in the spiritual combat against sin, and sustain us as we pray with conviction: *"Converte nos, Deus salutaris noster"* — "Convert us to you, O God, our salvation".

Walking in Lent

This is the First Sunday of Lent, the liturgical Season of 40 days which constitutes a spiritual journey in the Church of preparation for Easter. Essentially it is a matter of following Jesus who is walking with determination towards the Cross, the culmination of his mission of salvation. If we ask ourselves: "Why Lent? Why the Cross?", the answer in radical terms is this: because evil exists, indeed sin, which according to the Scriptures is the profound cause of all evil. However this affirmation is far from being taken for granted and the very word "sin" is not accepted by many because it implies a religious vision of the world and of the human being.

In fact it is true: if God is eliminated from the world's horizon, one cannot speak of sin. As when the sun is hidden, shadows disappear. Shadows only appear if the sun is out; hence the eclipse of God necessarily entails the eclipse of sin. Therefore the sense of sin — which is something different from the "sense of guilt" as psychology understands it — is acquired by rediscovering the sense of God. This is expressed by the *Miserere* Psalm, attributed to King David on the occasion of his double sin of adultery and homicide: "Against you",

David says, addressing God, "against you only have I sinned" (*Ps* 51(50):6).

He wants the sinner to convert and live

In the face of moral evil God's attitude is to oppose sin and to save the sinner. God does not tolerate evil because he is Love, Justice and Fidelity; and for this very reason he does not desire the death of the sinner but wants the sinner to convert and to live. To save humanity God intervenes: we see him throughout the history of the Jewish people, beginning with the liberation from Egypt. God is determined to deliver his children from slavery in order to lead them to freedom. And the most serious and profound slavery is precisely that of sin.

The definite plan of salvation

For this reason God sent his Son into the world: to set men and women free from the domination of Satan, "the origin and cause of every sin". God sent him in our mortal flesh so that he might become a victim of expiation, dying for us on the Cross. The Devil opposed this definitive and universal plan of salvation with all his might, as is shown in particular in the Gospel of the temptation of Jesus in the wilderness which is proclaimed every year on the First Sunday of Lent. In fact, entering this liturgical season means continuously taking Christ's side against sin, facing — both as individuals and as

Church — the spiritual fight against the spirit of evil each time *(Ash Wednesday, Opening Prayer)*.

Let us therefore invoke the maternal help of Mary Most Holy for the Lenten journey that has just begun, so that it may be rich in fruits of conversion.

The whole history of salvation illuminated

The Second Sunday of Lent, is called "of the Transfiguration" because the Gospel recounts this mystery of Jesus' life. After Jesus had foretold his Passion to the disciples, "he took with him Peter, James and John his brother, and led them up a high mountain apart. And he was transfigured before them, and his face shone like the sun, and his garments became white as light" *(Mt* 17:1-2). According to the senses the light of the sun is the brightest light known in nature but, according to the spirit, the disciples briefly glimpsed an even more intense splendour, that of the divine glory of Jesus which illumines the whole history of salvation. St Maximus Confessor says that "[the Lord's] garments appear white, that is to say, the words of the Gospel will then be clear and distinct, with nothing concealed" *(Ambiguum* 10: PG 91, 1128 B).

One dwelling place

The Gospel tells that beside the transfigured Jesus "there appeared... Moses and Elijah, talking with him" *(Mt* 17:3);

Moses and Elijah, figure of the Law and of the Prophets. It was then that Peter, ecstatic, exclaimed "Lord, it is well that we are here; if you wish, I will make three booths here, one for you and one for Moses and one for Elijah" (*Mt* 17:4). However St Augustine commented, saying that we have only one dwelling place, Christ: "he is the Word of God, the Word of God in the Law, the Word of God in the Prophets" (*Sermo De Verbis Ev.* 78:3: PL 38, 491).

In fact, the Father himself proclaims: "this is my beloved Son, with whom I am well pleased; listen to him" (*Mt* 17:5). The Transfiguration is not a change in Jesus but the revelation of his divinity: "the profound interpenetration of his being with God, which then becomes pure light. In his oneness with the Father, Jesus is himself 'light from light'" (*Jesus of Nazareth: From the Baptism in the Jordan to the Transfiguration*, Doubleday, New York, 2007, p. 310).

Ready to face the scandal of the cross

Peter, James and John, contemplating the divinity of the Lord, are ready to face the scandal of the Cross, as it is sung in an ancient hymn: "You were transfigured on the mountain and your disciples, insofar as they were able, contemplated your glory, in order that, on seeing you crucified, they would understand that your Passion was voluntary and proclaim to the world that you are truly the splendour of the Father" *(Κοντάκιον εἰς τήν Μεταμόρφωσιν*, in: *Μηναια,* t. 6, Rome 1901, 341).

A voluntary act

Let us too share in this vision and in this supernatural gift, making room for prayer, and for listening to the Word of God. Further, especially in this Season of Lent, I urge you, as the Servant of God Paul VI wrote, "to respond to the divine precept of penitence by some voluntary act, apart from the renunciation imposed by the burdens of everyday life" (Apostolic Constitution *Pœnitemini*, 17 February 1966, III, c: AAS 58 [1966], 182).

Let us invoke the Virgin Mary so that she may help us always to listen to and follow the Lord Jesus, even to the Passion and the Cross, in order to also participate in his glory.

He thirsted for the faith of us all

This third Sunday of Lent is characterized by the Jesus' famous conversation with the Samaritan woman, recounted by the Evangelist John. The woman went every day to draw water from an ancient well that dated back to the Patriarch Jacob and on that day she found Jesus sitting beside the well, "wearied from his journey" (Jn 4:6). St Augustine comments: "Not for nothing was Jesus tried... The strength of Christ created you, the weakness of Christ recreated you... With his strength he created us, with his weakness he came to seek us out" (*In Ioh. Ev.*, 15, 2).

Jesus' weariness, a sign of his true humanity, can be seen as a prelude to the Passion with which he brought to fulfilment the work of our redemption. In the encounter with the Samaritan woman at the well, the topic of Christ's "thirst" stands out in particular. It culminated in his cry on the Cross "I thirst" (*Jn* 19:28). This thirst, like his weariness, had a physical basis. Yet Jesus, as St Augustine says further, "thirsted for the faith of that woman" (*In Ioh. Ev.* 15,11), as he thirsted for the faith of us all.

Sent to quench our thirst for eternal life

God the Father sent him to quench our thirst for eternal life, giving us his love, but to give us this gift Jesus asks for our faith. The omnipotence of Love always respects human freedom; it knocks at the door of man's heart and waits patiently for his answer.

In the encounter with the Samaritan woman the symbol of water stands out in the foreground, alluding clearly to the sacrament of Baptism, the source of new life for faith in God's Grace. This Gospel, in fact — as I recalled in my Catechesis on Ash Wednesday — is part of the ancient journey of the catechumen's preparation for Christian Initiation, which took place at the great Easter

Vigil. "Whoever drinks of the water that I shall give him", Jesus said, "will never thirst; the water that I shall give him will become in him a spring of water welling up to eternal life" (*Jn* 4:14).

This water represents the Holy Spirit, the "gift" par excellence that Jesus came to bring on the part of God the Father. Whoever is reborn by water and by the Holy Spirit, that is, in Baptism, enters into a real relationship with God, a filial relationship, and can worship him "in spirit and in truth" (*Jn* 4:23, 24), as Jesus went on to reveal to the Samaritan woman. Thanks to the meeting with Jesus Christ and to the gift of the Holy Spirit, the human being's faith attains fulfilment, as a response to the fullness of God's revelation.

The appointment on which our true happiness depends

Each one of us can identify himself with the Samaritan woman: Jesus is waiting for us, especially in this Season of Lent, to speak to our hearts, to my heart. Let us pause a moment in silence, in our room or in a church or in a separate place. Let us listen to his voice which tells us "If you knew the gift of God…". May the Virgin Mary help us not to miss this appointment, on which our true happiness depends.

The profound light of realization

The Lenten journey that we are taking is a special time of grace during which we can experience the gift of the Lord's kindness to us. The Liturgy of this Sunday, called *"Laetare"*, invites us to be glad and rejoice as the Entrance Antiphon of the Eucharistic celebration proclaims: "Rejoice, Jerusalem! Be glad for her, you who love her; rejoice with her, you who mourned for her, and you will find contentment at her consoling breasts" (cf. *Is* 66: 10-11).

What is the profound reason for this joy? Today's Gospel in which Jesus heals a man blind from birth tells us. The question which the Lord Jesus asks the blind man is the high point of the story: "Do you believe in the Son of Man?" (*Jn* 9:35). The man recognizes the sign worked by Jesus and he passes from the light of his eyes to the light of faith: "Lord, I believe!" (*Jn* 9:38).

It should be noted that as a simple and sincere person he gradually completes the journey of faith. In the beginning he thinks of Jesus as a "man" among others, then he considers him a "prophet" and finally his eyes are opened and he proclaims him "Lord". In opposition to the faith of the healed blind man is the hardening of the hearts of the Pharisees who do not want to accept the miracle because they refuse to receive Jesus as the Messiah. Instead the crowd pauses to discuss the event and continues to be distant and indifferent. Even the blind man's parents are overcome by the fear of what others might think.

We too are born "blind"

And what attitude to Jesus should we adopt? Because of Adam's sin we too are born "blind" but in the baptismal font we are illumined by the grace of Christ. Sin wounded humanity and destined it to the darkness of death, but the newness of life shines out in Christ, as well as the destination to which we are called. In him, reinvigorated by the Holy Spirit, we receive the strength to defeat evil and to do good.

In fact the Christian life is a continuous conformation to Christ, image of the new man, in order to reach full communion with God. The Lord Jesus is the "light of the world" (*Jn* 8:12), because in him shines "the knowledge of the glory of God" (2 *Cor* 4:6) that continues in the complex plot of the story to reveal the meaning of human existence.

The joy of realization

In the rite of Baptism, the presentation of the candle lit from the large Paschal candle, a symbol of the Risen Christ, is a sign that helps us to understand what happens in the Sacrament. When our lives are enlightened by the mystery of Christ, we experience the joy of being liberated from all that threatens the full realization.

In these days which prepare us for Easter let us rekindle within us the gift received in Baptism, that flame which sometimes risks being extinguished. Let us nourish it with prayer and love for others. Let us entrust our Lenten journey to the Virgin Mary, Mother of the Church so that all may encounter Christ, Saviour of the world.

Our own resurrection

There are only two weeks to go until Easter and the Bible Readings of this Sunday all speak about resurrection. It is not yet that of Jesus, which bursts in as an absolute innovation, but our own resurrection, to which we aspire and which Christ himself gave to us, in rising from the dead. Indeed, death represents a wall as it were, which prevents us from seeing beyond it; yet our hearts reach out beyond this wall and even though we cannot understand what it conceals, we nevertheless think about it and imagine it, expressing with symbols our desire for eternity.

The Prophet Ezekiel proclaimed to the Jewish people, exiled far from the land of Israel, that God would open the graves of the dead and bring them home to rest in peace (cf. *Ezek* 37:12-14). This ancestral aspiration of man to be buried together with his forefathers is the longing for a "homeland" which welcomes us at the end of our earthly toil. This concept does not yet contain the idea of a personal resurrection from death, which only appears towards the end of the Old Testament, and even in Jesus' time was not accepted by all Judeans. Among Christians too, faith in the resurrection and in life is often accompanied by many doubts and much confusion because it also always concerns a reality which goes beyond the limits of our reason and requires an act of faith.

Full dominion over physical death

In today's Gospel — the raising of Lazarus — we listen to the voice of faith from the lips of Martha, Lazarus' sister. Jesus said to her: "Your brother will rise again," and she replies: "I know that he will rise again in the resurrection at the last day" (*Jn* 11:23-24). But Jesus repeats: "I am the resurrection and the life; he who believes in me, though he die, yet shall he live" (*Jn* 11:25-26). This is the true newness which abounds and exceeds every border! Christ pulls down the wall of death and in him dwells all the fullness of God, who is life, eternal life. Therefore death did not have power over him and the raising of Lazarus is a sign of his full dominion over physical death which, before God, resembles sleep (cf. *Jn* 11:11).

Spiritual death and sin

However there is another death, which cost Christ the hardest struggle, even the price of the Cross: it is spiritual death and sin which threaten to ruin the existence of every human being. To overcome *this* death, Christ died and his Resurrection is not a return to past life, but an opening to a new reality, a "new land" united at last with God's Heaven. Therefore St Paul writes: "If the Spirit of him who raised Jesus from the dead dwells in you, he who raised Christ Jesus from he dead will give life to your mortal bodies also through his Spirit who dwells in you" (*Rom* 8:11).

Let us turn to the Virgin Mary, who previously shared in this Resurrection, so that she may help us to say faithfully: "Yes, Lord; I believe that you are the Christ, the Son of God" (*Jn* 11:27), to truly discover that he is our salvation.

Road that leads to the living God – Palm Sunday

It is a moving experience each year on Palm Sunday as we go up the mountain with Jesus, towards the Temple, accompanying him on his ascent. On this day, throughout the world and across the centuries, young people and people of every age acclaim him, crying out: "Hosanna to the Son of David! Blessed is he who comes in the name of the Lord!"

But what are we really doing when we join this procession as part of the throng which went up with Jesus to Jerusalem and hailed him as King of Israel? Is this anything more than a ritual, a quaint custom? Does it have anything to do with the reality of our life and our world? To answer this, we must first be clear about what Jesus himself wished to do and actually did. After Peter's confession of faith in Caesarea Philippi, in the northernmost part of the Holy Land, Jesus set out as a pilgrim towards Jerusalem for the feast of Passover. He was journeying towards the Temple in the Holy City, towards that place which for Israel ensured in a particular way God's closeness to his people. He was making his way towards the common feast of Passover, the memorial of Israel's liberation from Egypt and the sign of its hope of definitive liberation. He knew that what awaited him was a new Passover and that he himself would take the place of the sacrificial lambs by offering himself on the cross. He knew that in the mysterious gifts of bread and wine he would give himself for ever to his own, and that he would open to them the door to a new path of liberation, to fellowship with the living God. He was making his way to the heights of the Cross, to the moment of self-giving love. The ultimate goal of his pilgrimage was the heights of God himself; to those heights he wanted to lift every human being.

Our procession today is meant, then, to be an image of something deeper, to reflect the fact that, together with Jesus, we are setting out on pilgrimage along the high road that leads to the living God. This is the ascent that matters. This is the journey which Jesus invites us to make. But how can we keep pace with this ascent? Isn't it beyond our ability? Certainly, it is beyond our own possibilities. From the beginning men and women have been filled – and this is as true today as ever – with a desire to "be like God", to attain the heights of God by their own powers. All the inventions of the human spirit are ultimately an effort to gain wings so as to rise to the heights of Being and to become independent, completely free, as God is free. Mankind has managed to accomplish so many things: we can fly! We can see, hear and speak to one another from the farthest ends of the earth. And yet the force of gravity which draws us down is powerful. With the increase of our abilities there has been an increase not only of good. Our possibilities for evil have increased and appear like menacing storms above history. Our limitations have also remained: we need but think of the disasters which have caused so much suffering for humanity in recent months.

Escaping the gravitational field of evil

The Fathers of the Church maintained that human beings stand at the point of intersection between two gravitational fields. First, there is the force of gravity which pulls us down – towards selfishness, falsehood and evil; the gravity which diminishes us and distances us from the heights of God. On the other hand there is the gravitational force of God's love: the fact that we are loved by God and respond in love attracts us upwards. Man finds himself betwixt this twofold gravitational force; everything depends on our escaping the gravitational field of evil and becoming free to be attracted completely by the gravitational force of God, which makes us authentic, elevates us and grants us true freedom.

God himself must draw us up

Following the Liturgy of the Word, at the beginning of the Eucharistic Prayer where the Lord comes into our midst, the Church invites us to lift up our hearts: *"Sursum corda!"* In the language of the Bible and the thinking of the Fathers, the heart is the centre of man, where understanding, will and feeling, body and soul, all come together. The centre where spirit becomes body and body becomes spirit, where will, feeling and understanding become one in the knowledge and love of God. This is the "heart" which must be lifted up. But to repeat: of ourselves, we are too weak to lift up our hearts to the heights of God. We cannot do it. The very pride of thinking that we are able to do it on our own drags us down and estranges us from God. God himself must draw us up, and this is what Christ began to do on the cross. He descended to the depths of our human existence in order to draw us up to himself, to the living God. He humbled himself, as today's second reading says. Only in this way could our pride be vanquished: God's humility is the extreme form of his love, and this humble love draws us upwards.

The song of ascent

Psalm 24, which the Church proposes as the "song of ascent" to accompany our procession in today's liturgy, indicates some concrete elements which are part of our ascent and without which we cannot be lifted upwards: clean hands, a pure heart, the rejection of falsehood, the quest for God's face. The great achievements of technology are liberating and contribute to the progress of mankind only if they are joined to these attitudes – if our hands become clean and our hearts pure, if we seek truth, if we seek God and let ourselves be touched and challenged by his love. All these means of "ascent" are effective only if we humbly acknowledge that we need to be lifted up; if we abandon the pride of wanting to become God. We need God: he draws us upwards; letting ourselves be upheld by his hands – by faith, in other words – sets us aright and gives us the inner strength that raises us on high. We need the humility of a faith which seeks the face of God and trusts in the truth of his love.

How man can attain the heights

The question of how man can attain the heights, becoming completely himself and completely like God, has always engaged mankind. It was passionately disputed by the Platonic philosophers of the third and fourth centuries. For them, the central issue was finding the means of purification which could free man from the heavy load weighing him down and thus enable him to ascend to the heights of his true being, to the heights of divinity. Saint Augustine, in his search for the right path, long sought guidance from those philosophies. But in the end he had to acknowledge that their answers were insufficient, their methods would not truly lead him to God. To those philosophers he said: recognize that human power and all these purifications are not enough to bring man in truth to the heights of the divine, to his own heights. And he added that he should have despaired of himself and human existence had he not found the One who accomplishes what we of ourselves cannot accomplish; the One who raises us up to the heights of God in spite of our wretchedness: Jesus Christ who from God came down to us and, in his crucified love, takes us by the hand and lifts us on high.

Seeking the face of God

We are on pilgrimage with the Lord to the heights. We are striving for pure hearts and clean hands, we are seeking truth, we are seeking the face of God. Let us show the Lord that we desire to be righteous, and let us ask him: Draw us upwards! Make us pure! Grant that the words which we sang in the processional psalm may also hold true for us; grant that we may be part of the generation which seeks God, "which seeks your face, O God of Jacob" (cf. *Ps* 24:6).

He makes us all one – the Lord's Supper

"I have eagerly desired to eat this Passover with you before I suffer" (*Lk* 22:15). With these words Jesus began the celebration of his final meal and the institution of the Holy Eucharist. Jesus approached that hour with eager desire. In his heart he awaited the moment when he would give himself to his own under the appearance of bread and wine. He awaited that moment which would in some sense be the true messianic wedding feast: when he would transform the gifts of this world and become one with his own, so as to transform them and thus inaugurate the transformation of the world.

An expectant love for mankind

In this eager desire of Jesus we can recognize the desire of God himself – his expectant love for mankind, for his creation. A love which awaits the moment of union, a love which wants to draw mankind to itself and thereby fulfil the desire of all creation, for creation eagerly awaits the revelation of the children of God (cf. *Rom* 8:19). Jesus desires us, he awaits us. But what about ourselves? Do we really desire him? Are we anxious to meet him? Do we desire to encounter him, to become one with him, to receive the gifts he offers us in the Holy Eucharist? Or are we indifferent, distracted, busy about other things? From Jesus' banquet parables we realize that he knows all about empty places at table, invitations refused, lack of interest in him and his closeness. For us, the empty places at the table of the Lord's wedding feast, whether excusable or not, are no longer a parable but a reality, in those very countries to which he had revealed his closeness in a special way.

Faith requires love or it is dead

Jesus also knew about guests who come to the banquet without being robed in the wedding garment – they come not to rejoice in his presence but merely out of habit, since their hearts are elsewhere. In one of his homilies Saint Gregory the Great asks: Who are these people who enter without the wedding garment? What is this garment and how does one acquire it? He replies that those who are invited and enter do in some way have faith. It is faith which opens the door to them. But they lack the wedding garment of love. Those who do not live their faith as love are not ready for the banquet and are cast out. Eucharistic communion requires faith, but faith requires love; otherwise, even as faith, it is dead.

The upward movement of thanking and the downward movement of blessing go together

From all four Gospels we know that Jesus' final meal before his passion was also a teaching moment. Once again, Jesus urgently set forth the heart of his message. Word and sacrament, message and gift are inseparably linked. Yet at his final meal, more than anything else, Jesus prayed. Matthew, Mark and Luke use two words in describing Jesus' prayer at the culmination of the meal: *"eucharístesas"* and *"eulógesas"* – the verbs "to give thanks" and "to bless".

The upward movement of thanking and the downward movement of blessing go together. The words of transubstantiation are part of this prayer of Jesus. They are themselves words of prayer. Jesus turns his suffering into prayer, into an offering to the Father for the sake of mankind.

This transformation of his suffering into love has the power to transform the gifts in which he now gives himself. He gives those gifts to us, so that we, and our world, may be transformed. The ultimate purpose of Eucharistic transformation is our own transformation in communion with Christ. The Eucharist is directed to the new man, the new world, which can only come about from God, through the ministry of God's Servant.

The prayer for unity

From Luke, and especially from John, we know that Jesus, during the Last Supper, also prayed to the Father – prayers which also contain a plea to his disciples of that time and of all times. Here I would simply like to take one of these which, as John tells us, Jesus repeated four times in his Priestly Prayer. How deeply it must have concerned him! It remains his constant prayer to the Father on our behalf: the prayer for unity. Jesus explicitly states that this prayer is not meant simply for the disciples then present, but for all who would believe in him (cf. *Jn* 17:20). He prays that all may be one "as you, Father, are in me and I am in you, so that the world may believe" (*Jn* 17:21).

Christian unity can exist only if Christians are deeply united to him, to Jesus. Faith and love for Jesus, faith in his being one with the Father and openness to becoming one with him, are essential. This unity, then, is not something purely interior or mystical. It must become visible, so visible as to prove before the world that Jesus was sent by the Father. Consequently, Jesus' prayer has an underlying Eucharistic meaning which Paul clearly brings out in the First Letter to the Corinthians: "The bread that we break, is it not a sharing in the body of Christ? Because there is one bread, we who are many, are one body, for we all partake of the one bread" (1 *Cor* 10:16ff.).

With the Eucharist, the Church is born. All of us eat the one bread and receive the one body of the Lord; this means that he opens each of us up to something above and beyond us. He makes all of us one. The Eucharist is the mystery of the profound closeness and communion of each individual with the Lord and, at the same time, of visible union between all. The Eucharist is the sacrament of unity. It reaches the very mystery of the Trinity and thus creates visible unity.

Let me say it again: it is an extremely personal encounter with the Lord and yet never simply an act of individual piety. Of necessity, we celebrate it together. In each community the Lord is totally present. Yet in all the communities he is but one. Hence the words *"una cum Papa nostro et cum episcopo nostro"* are a requisite part of the Church's Eucharistic Prayer. These words are not an addendum of sorts, but a necessary expression of what the Eucharist really is. Furthermore, we mention the Pope and the Bishop by name: unity is something utterly concrete, it has names. In this way unity becomes visible; it becomes a sign for the world and a concrete criterion for ourselves.

The constant need of conversion

Saint Luke has preserved for us one concrete element of Jesus' prayer for unity: "Simon, Simon, behold, Satan demanded to have you, that he might sift you like wheat, but I have prayed for you, that your faith may not fail; and when you have turned again, strengthen your brethren" (*Lk* 22:31). Today we are once more painfully aware that Satan has been permitted to sift the disciples before the whole world. And we know that Jesus prays for the faith of Peter and his successors. We know that Peter, who walks towards the Lord upon the stormy waters of history and is in danger of sinking, is sustained ever anew by the Lord's hand and guided over the waves. But Jesus continues with a prediction and a mandate. "When you have turned again…" Every human being, save Mary, has constant need of conversion.

We must discover our humility ever anew

Jesus tells Peter beforehand of his coming betrayal and conversion. But what did Peter need to be converted from? When first called, terrified by the Lord's divine power and his own weakness, Peter had said: "Go away from me, Lord, for I am a sinful man!" (*Lk* 5:8). In the light of the Lord, he recognizes his own inadequacy. Precisely in this way, in the humility of one who knows that he is a sinner, is he called. He must discover this humility ever anew. At Caesarea Philippi Peter could not accept that Jesus would have to suffer and be crucified: it did not fit his image of God and the Messiah. In the Upper Room he did not want Jesus to wash his feet: it did not fit his image of the dignity of the Master. In the

52

Garden of Olives he wielded his sword. He wanted to show his courage. Yet before the servant girl he declared that he did not know Jesus. At the time he considered it a little lie which would let him stay close to Jesus. All his heroism collapsed in a shabby bid to be at the centre of things. We too, all of us, need to learn again to accept God and Jesus Christ as he is, and not the way we want him to be. We too find it hard to accept that he bound himself to the limitations of his Church and her ministers. We too do not want to accept that he is powerless in this world. We too find excuses when being his disciples starts becoming too costly, too dangerous. All of us need the conversion which enables us to accept Jesus in his reality as God and man. We need the humility of the disciple who follows the will of his Master. Tonight we want to ask Jesus to look to us, as with kindly eyes he looked to Peter when the time was right, and to convert us.

Called to strength through prayer and desire for the Lord

After Peter was converted, he was called to strengthen his brethren. It is not irrelevant that this task was entrusted to him in the Upper Room. The ministry of unity has its visible place in the celebration of the Holy Eucharist. Dear friends, it is a great consolation for the Pope to know that at each Eucharistic celebration everyone prays for him, and that our prayer is joined to the Lord's prayer for Peter. Only by the prayer of the Lord and of the Church can the Pope fulfil his task of strengthening his brethren – of feeding the flock of Christ and of becoming the guarantor of that unity which becomes a visible witness to the mission which Jesus received from the Father.

"I have eagerly desired to eat this Passover with you". Lord, you desire us, you desire me. You eagerly desire to share yourself with us in the Holy Eucharist, to be one with us. Lord, awaken in us the desire for you. Strengthen us in unity with you and with one another. Grant unity to your Church, so that the world may believe.

Way of the Cross – Good Friday

This evening, in faith, we have accompanied Jesus as he takes the final steps of his earthly journey, the most painful steps, the steps that lead to Calvary. We have heard the cries of the crowd, the words of condemnation, the insults of the soldiers, the lamentation of the Virgin Mary and of the women. Now we are immersed in the silence of this night, in the silence of the cross, the silence of death. It is a silence pregnant with the burden of pain borne by a man rejected, oppressed, downtrodden, the burden of sin which mars his face, the burden of evil. Tonight we have re-lived, deep within our hearts, the drama of Jesus, weighed down by pain, by evil, by human sin.

What remains now before our eyes? It is a crucified man, a cross raised on Golgotha, a cross which seems a sign of the final defeat of the One who brought light to those immersed in darkness, the One who spoke of the power of forgiveness and of mercy, the One who asked us to believe in God's infinite love for each human person. Despised and rejected by men, there stands before us "a man of suffering and acquainted with infirmity, one from whom others hide their faces" (*Is* 53:3).

The Cross is a luminous sign of love

But let us look more closely at that man crucified between earth and heaven. Let us contemplate him more intently, and we will realize that the cross is not the banner of the victory of death, sin and evil, but rather the luminous sign of love, of God's immense love, of something that we could never have asked, imagined or expected: God bent down over us, he lowered himself, even to the darkest corner of our lives, in order to stretch out his hand and draw us to himself, to bring us all the way to himself. The cross speaks to us of the supreme love of God and invites, today, to renew our faith in the power of that love, and to believe that in every situation of our lives, our history and our world, God is able to vanquish death, sin and evil, and to give us new, risen life. In the Son of God's death on the cross, we find the seed of new hope for life, like the seed which dies within the earth.

A night full of silence and hope

This night full of silence, full of hope, echoes God's call to us as found in the words of Saint Augustine: "Have faith! You will come to me and you will taste the good things of my table, even as I did not disdain to taste the evil things of your table... I have promised you my own life. As a pledge of this, I have given you my death, as if to say: Look! I am inviting you to share in my life. It is a life where no one dies, a life which is truly blessed, which offers an incorruptible food, the food which refreshes and never fails. The goal to which I invite you... is friendship with the Father and the Holy Spirit, it is the eternal supper, it is communion with me... It is a share in my own life (cf. *Sermo* 231, 5).

Let us gaze on the crucified Jesus, and let us ask in prayer: Enlighten our hearts, Lord, that we may follow you along the way of the cross. Put to death in us the "old man" bound by selfishness, evil and sin. Make us "new men", men and women of holiness, transformed and enlivened by your love.

Reason and freedom in creation – Easter Vigil

The liturgical celebration of the Easter Vigil makes use of two eloquent signs. First there is the fire that becomes light. As the procession makes its way through the church, shrouded in the darkness of the night, the light of the Paschal Candle becomes a wave of lights, and it speaks to us of Christ as the true morning star that never sets – the Risen Lord in whom light has conquered darkness. The second sign is water. On the one hand, it recalls the waters of the Red Sea, decline and death, the mystery of the Cross. But now it is presented to us as spring water, a life-giving element amid the dryness. Thus it becomes the image of the sacrament of baptism, through which we become sharers in the death and resurrection of Jesus Christ.

Yet these great signs of creation, light and water, are not the only constituent elements of the liturgy of the Easter Vigil. Another essential feature is the ample encounter with the words of sacred Scripture that it provides. Before the liturgical reform there were twelve Old Testament readings and two from the New Testament. The New Testament readings have been retained. The number of Old Testament readings has been fixed at seven, but depending upon the local situation, they may be reduced to three. The Church wishes to offer us a panoramic view of whole trajectory of salvation history, starting with creation, passing through the election and the liberation of Israel to the testimony of the prophets by which this entire history is directed ever more clearly towards Jesus Christ. In the liturgical tradition all these readings were called prophecies. Even when they are not directly foretelling future events, they have a prophetic character, they show us the inner foundation and orientation of history. They cause creation and history to become transparent to what is essential. In this way they take us by the hand and lead us towards Christ, they show us the true Light.

The creation story is itself a prophecy

At the Easter Vigil, the journey along the paths of sacred Scripture begins with the account of creation. This is the liturgy's way of telling us that the creation story is itself a prophecy. It is not information about the external processes by which the cosmos and man himself came into being. The Fathers of the Church were well aware of this. They did not interpret the story as an account of the process of the origins of things, but rather as a pointer towards the essential, towards the true beginning and end of our being. Now, one might ask: is it really important to speak also of creation during the Easter Vigil? Could we not begin with the events in which God calls man, forms a people for himself and creates his history with men upon the earth? The answer has to be: no. To omit the creation would be to misunderstand the very history of God with men, to diminish it, to lose sight of its true order of greatness. The sweep of history established by God reaches back to the origins, back to creation.

Our profession of faith begins with the words: "We believe in God, the Father Almighty, Creator of heaven and earth". If we omit the beginning of the *Credo*, the whole history of salvation becomes too limited and too small. The Church is not some kind of association that concerns itself with man's religious needs but is limited to that objective. No, she brings man into contact with God and thus with the source of all things. Therefore we relate to God as Creator, and so we have a responsibility for creation. Our responsibility extends as far as creation because it comes from the Creator. Only because God created everything can he give us life and direct our lives. Life in the Church's faith involves more than a set of feelings and sentiments and perhaps moral obligations. It embraces man in his entirety, from his origins to his eternal destiny. Only because creation belongs to God can we place ourselves completely in his hands. And only because he is the Creator can he give us life for ever. Joy over creation, thanksgiving for creation and responsibility for it all belong together.

The world is a product of creative reason

The central message of the creation account can be defined more precisely still. In the opening words of his Gospel, Saint John sums up the essential meaning of that account in this single statement: "In the beginning was the Word". In effect, the creation account that we listened to earlier is characterized by the regularly recurring phrase: "And God said ..." The world is a product of the Word, of the *Logos*, as Saint John expresses it, using a key term from the Greek language. *"Logos"* means "reason", "sense", "word". It is not reason pure and simple, but creative Reason, that speaks and communicates itself. It is Reason that both is and creates sense. The creation account tells us, then, that the world is a product of creative Reason. Hence it tells us that, far from there being an absence of reason and freedom at the origin of all things, the source of everything is creative Reason, love, and freedom.

In the beginning is reason and freedom

Here we are faced with the ultimate alternative that is at stake in the dispute between faith and unbelief: are irrationality, lack of freedom and pure chance the origin of everything, or are reason, freedom and love at the origin of being? Does the primacy belong to unreason or to reason? This is what everything hinges upon in the final analysis. As believers we answer, with the creation account and with Saint John, that in the beginning is reason. In the beginning is freedom. Hence it is good to be a human person. It is not the case that in the expanding universe, at a late stage, in some tiny corner of the cosmos, there evolved randomly some species of living being capable of reasoning and of trying to find rationality within creation, or to bring rationality into it. If man were merely a random product of evolution in some place on the margins of the universe, then his life would make no sense or might even be a chance of nature. But no, Reason is there at the beginning: creative, divine Reason. And because it is Reason, it also created freedom; and because freedom can be abused, there also exist forces harmful to creation. Hence a thick black line, so to speak, has been drawn across the structure of the universe and across the nature of man. But despite this contradiction, creation itself remains good, life remains good, because at the beginning is good Reason, God's creative love. Hence the world can be saved. Hence we can and must place ourselves on the side of reason, freedom and love – on the side of God who loves us so much that he suffered for us, that from his death there might emerge a new, definitive and healed life.

The Covenant is inbuilt at the deepest level of creation

The Old Testament account of creation that we listened to clearly indicates this order of realities. But it leads us a further step forward. It has structured the process of creation within the framework of a week leading up to the Sabbath, in which it finds its completion. For Israel, the Sabbath was the day on which all could participate in God's rest, in which man and animal, master and slave, great and small were united in God's freedom. Thus the Sabbath was an expression of the Covenant between God and man and creation. In this way, communion between God and man does not appear as something extra, something added later to a world already fully created. The Covenant, communion between God and man, is inbuilt at the deepest level of creation. Yes, the Covenant is the inner ground of creation, just as creation is the external presupposition of the Covenant. God made the world so that there could be a space where he might communicate his love, and from which the response of love might come back to him. From God's perspective, the heart of the man who responds to him is greater and more important than the whole immense material cosmos, for all that the latter allows us to glimpse something of God's grandeur.

The day of the new creation

Easter and the paschal experience of Christians, however, now require us to take a further step. The Sabbath is the seventh day of the week. After six days in which man in some sense participates in God's work of creation, the

Sabbath is the day of rest. But something quite unprecedented happened in the nascent Church: the place of the Sabbath, the seventh day, was taken by the first day. As the day of the liturgical assembly, it is the day for encounter with God through Jesus Christ who as the Risen Lord encountered his followers on the first day, Sunday, after they had found the tomb empty. The structure of the week is overturned. No longer does it point towards the seventh day, as the time to participate in God's rest. It sets out from the first day as the day of encounter with the Risen Lord. This encounter happens afresh at every celebration of the Eucharist, when the Lord enters anew into the midst of his disciples and gives himself to them, allows himself, so to speak, to be touched by them, sits down at table with them. This change is utterly extraordinary, considering that the Sabbath, the seventh day seen as the day of encounter with God, is so profoundly rooted in the Old Testament. If we also bear in mind how much the movement from work towards the rest-day corresponds to a natural rhythm, the dramatic nature of this change is even more striking. This revolutionary development that occurred at the very the beginning of the Church's history can be explained only by the fact that something utterly new happened that day. The first day of the week was the third day after Jesus' death. It was the day when he showed himself to his disciples as the Risen Lord. In truth, this encounter had something unsettling about it. The world had changed. This man who had died was now living with a life that was no longer threatened by any death. A new form of life had been inaugurated, a new dimension of creation. The first day, according to the Genesis account, is the day on which creation begins. Now it was the day of creation in a new way, it had become the day of the new creation. We celebrate the first day. And in so doing we celebrate God the Creator and his creation. Yes, we believe in God, the Creator of heaven and earth. And we celebrate the God who was made man, who suffered, died, was buried and rose again. We celebrate the definitive victory of the Creator and of his creation. We celebrate this day as the origin and the goal of our existence. We celebrate it because now, thanks to the risen Lord, it is definitively established that reason is stronger than unreason, truth stronger than lies, love stronger than death. We celebrate the first day because we know that the black line drawn across creation does not last for ever. We celebrate it because we know that those words from the end of the creation account have now been definitively fulfilled: "God saw everything that he had made, and behold, it was very good" (*Gen* 1:31).

Continuous resurrection within us – Octave of Easter

In these first days of the Easter Season — which lasts until Pentecost — we are still filled with the freshness and new joy that the liturgical celebrations have brought to our hearts. I would therefore like to reflect briefly with you on Easter, the heart of the Christian mystery. Everything, in fact, starts here: our faith is founded on Christ risen from the dead.

The whole liturgy of the Church radiates from Easter, as if from a luminous, incandescent centre, drawing from it content and significance. The liturgical celebration of the death and Resurrection of Christ is not a simple commemoration of this event but is its actualization in the mystery, for the life of every Christian and of every ecclesial community, for our life. In fact, faith in the Risen Christ transforms life, bringing about within us a continuous resurrection, as St Paul wrote to the first believers: "For once you were darkness, but now you are light in the Lord; walk as children of light (for the fruit of light is found in all that is good and right and true)" (*Eph* 5:8-9).

So how can we make Easter become "life"? How can the whole of our interior and exterior existence take on a paschal "form"? We must start from an authentic understanding of Jesus' Resurrection: this event is not merely a return to previous life, as it was for Lazarus, for the daughter of Jairus and for the young man of Nain; rather it is something entirely new and different.

A life steeped in God's eternity

Christ's Resurrection is a landing place on the way to a life no longer subjected to the transience of time, a life steeped in God's eternity. In the Resurrection of Jesus a new condition of being human begins, which illumines and transforms our daily routine and opens a qualitatively different and new future to humanity as a whole.

For this reason not only does St Paul interpret the resurrection of Christians in a manner inseparable from that of Jesus (cf. 1 *Cor* 15:16, 20), but he also points out how we should live the Paschal Mystery in our everyday lives.

In the Letter to the Colossians, he says: "If then you have been raised with Christ, seek the things that are above, where Christ is, seated at the right hand of God. Set your minds on things that are above, not on things that are on earth" (3:1-2). At first sight, on reading this text it might seem that the Apostle intends to encourage contempt of earthly realities, in other words inviting us to forget this world of suffering, injustice and sin, in order to live in anticipation in a heavenly paradise. The thought of

"Heaven" would in this case be a sort of alienation. Yet, to grasp the true meaning of these Pauline affirmations, it is sufficient not to separate them from the context. The Apostle explains very clearly what he means by "things that are above" which the Christian must seek and the "things that are on earth", that the Christian should avoid.

Earthly things that must be avoided

Now, first of all what are the "things of the earth" that must be avoided? "Put to death therefore", St Paul writes, "what is earthly in you: immorality, impurity, passion, evil desire, and covetousness, which is idolatry" (3:5-6). Putting to death within us the insatiable desire for material goods, selfishness, the root of all sin. Therefore, when the Apostle invites Christians to detach themselves firmly from the "things of the earth", he clearly wishes to make them understand that they belong to the "old nature", from which the Christian must divest himself, in order to put on Christ.

Things we must seek and savour

Just as he was unambivalent in spelling out the things which we should not set our hearts on, he was equally clear in pointing out to us the "things that are above", which on the contrary Christians must seek and savour. They concern what belongs to the "new nature", which has put on Christ once and for all in Baptism, but always needs to be renewed "after the image of its Creator" (*Col* 3:10). This is how the Apostle to the Gentiles describes these "things that are above": "Put on then, as God's chosen ones, holy and beloved, compassion, kindness, lowliness, meekness, and patience, forbearing one another and, if one has a complaint against another, forgiving each other.... And above all these put on love, which binds everything together in perfect harmony" (*Col* 3:12-24).

Live as new men and women

St Paul, therefore is very far from inviting Christians, each one of us, to escape from the world in which God has placed us. It is true that we are citizens of another "city", where our true homeland is found; but we must journey on towards this destination every day, here on earth. Taking part from this moment in the life of the Risen Christ, we must live in this world, in the heart of the earthly city, as new men and women.

Virtues that must accompany Christian life

And this is not only the way to transform ourselves, but also to transform the world, to give the earthly city a new face that will encourage the development of humanity and of society, in accordance with the logic of solidarity, of goodness, in profound respect for the dignity proper to each one. The Apostle reminds us of the virtues that must accompany Christian life; at the top of the list is charity, to which all the others are related, as to the source and the matrix. Christian life sums up or summarizes the "things that are in Heaven": charity, which, with faith and hope, represents the great rule of life of the Christian and defines its profound nature.

A life of freedom

Easter, therefore, brings the newness of a profound and total passage from a life subjected to the slavery of sin to a life of freedom, enlivened by love, a force that pulls down every barrier and builds a new harmony in one's own heart and in the relationship with others and with things. Every Christian just as every community, if he lives the experience of this passage of resurrection, cannot but be a new leaven in the world, giving himself without reserve for the most urgent and just causes, as the testimonies of the saints in every epoch and in every place show.

Luminous witnesses every day

The expectations of our time are so numerous: we Christians, firmly believing that Christ's Resurrection has renewed man without taking him from the world in which he builds his history, we must be luminous witnesses of this new life that Easter has brought.

Easter is therefore a gift to be accepted ever more deeply in the faith, to be able to operate in every situation with the grace of Christ, according to the logic of God, the logic of love. The light of Christ's Resurrection must penetrate this world of ours; as a message of truth and life it must reach all human beings through our daily witness.

Yes, Christ is truly risen! We cannot keep for ourselves the life and joy that he has given us in his Passover, but rather we must give it to all who approach us. It is our duty and our mission: to kindle in the heart of our neighbour hope where there is despair, joy where there is sorrow, life where there is death.

Witnessing every day to the joy of the Risen Lord means always living in "a paschal mode" and causing to ring out the Good News that Christ is neither an idea nor a memory of the past, but a Person who lives with us, for us and in us, and with him, for him and in him we can make all things new (cf. *Rev* 21:5).

The gift of joy itself – Pentecost

Today we are celebrating the great Solemnity of Pentecost. If, in a certain sense, all the liturgical solemnities of the Church are important, Pentecost is uniquely so. This is because, having reached the 50th day, it marks the fulfilment of the event of the passover, death and resurrection of the Lord Jesus through the gift of the Spirit of the Risen One. In the past few days the Church has prepared us for Pentecost with her prayer, with her repeated and intense invocation to God to obtain a fresh outpouring upon us of the Holy Spirit. The Church has thus relived all that happened at her origins, when the Apostles gathered in the Upper Room of Jerusalem "with one accord devoted themselves to prayer, together with the women and Mary the Mother of Jesus, and with his brethren" (*Acts* 1:14).

They were gathered in humble and trusting expectation that the Father's promise, announced to them by Jesus, would be fulfilled: "Before many days you shall be baptized with the Holy Spirit... you shall receive power when the Holy Spirit has come upon you" (*Acts* 1:5,8).

The revealed face of God

The liturgy of the Pentecost Psalm 104[103], corresponds with the account in the Acts of the Apostles of the birth of the Church (cf. *Acts* 2:1-11): a hymn of praise of the whole creation which exalts the Creator Spirit who has made all things with wisdom: "O Lord, how manifold are your works! In wisdom you have made them all; the earth is full of your creatures... May the glory of the Lord endure for ever, may the Lord rejoice in his works" (*Ps* 104[103]:24, 31). This is what the Church wants to tell us: the Spirit Creator of all things and the Holy Spirit whom the Lord caused to come down from the Father upon the community of the disciples are one and the same. Creation and redemption belong to each other and constitute, in depth, one mystery of love and of salvation. The Holy Spirit is first and foremost a Creator Spirit, hence Pentecost is also a feast of creation. For us Christians, the world is the fruit of an act of love by God who has made all things and in which he rejoices because it is "good", it is "very good", as the creation narrative tells us (cf. *Gen* 1:1-31). Consequently God is not totally Other, unnameable and obscure. God reveals himself, he has a face. God is reason, God is will, God is love, God is beauty. Faith in the Creator Spirit and faith in the Spirit whom the Risen Christ gave to the Apostles and gives to each one of us are therefore inseparably united.

Multiplicity becomes a multi-faceted unity

The Second Reading and Gospel show us this connection. The Holy Spirit is the One who makes us recognize the Lord in Christ and prompts us to speak the profession of the Church's faith: "Jesus is Lord" (cf. 1 *Co* 12:3b). "Lord" is the title attributed to God in the Old Testament, a title that in the interpretation of the Bible replaced his unpronounceable name. The *Creed* of the Church is nothing other than the development of what we say with this simple affirmation: "Jesus is Lord". Concerning this profession of faith St Paul tells us that it is precisely a matter of the word and work of the Spirit. If we want to be in the Spirit, we must adhere to this *Creed*. By making it our own, by accepting it as our word we gain access to the work of the Holy Spirit. The words "Jesus is Lord" can be interpreted in two ways. They mean: Jesus is God, and, at the same time: God is Jesus. The Holy Spirit illuminates this reciprocity: Jesus has divine dignity and God has the human face of Jesus. God shows himself in Jesus and by doing so gives us the truth about ourselves. Letting ourselves be enlightened by this word in the depths of our inmost being is the event of Pentecost. In reciting the *Creed* we enter into the mystery of the first Pentecost: a radical transformation results from the tumult of Babel, from those voices yelling at each other: multiplicity becomes a multi-faceted unity, understanding grows from the unifying power of the Truth. In the *Creed*

— which unites us from all the corners of the earth and which, through the Holy Spirit, ensures that we understand each other even in the diversity of languages — the new community of God's Church is formed through faith, hope and love.

The Lord breathes a breath of life into our Soul

The Gospel passage then offers us a marvellous image to clarify the connection between Jesus, the Holy Spirit and the Father: the Holy Spirit is portrayed as the breath of the Risen Jesus Christ (cf. *Jn* 20:22). Here the Evangelist John takes up an image of the creation narrative, where it says that God breathed into the nostrils of man the breath of life (cf. *Gen* 2:7). The breath of God is life. Now, the Lord breathes into our soul the new breath of life, the Holy Spirit, his most intimate essence, and in this way welcomes us into God's family. With Baptism and Confirmation this gift was given to us specifically, and with the sacraments of the Eucharist and Penance it is continuously repeated: the Lord breathes a breath of life into our soul. All the sacraments, each in its own way, communicate divine life to human beings, thanks to the Holy Spirit who works within them.

Pentecost as a new Sinai

In today's liturgy we perceive another connection. The Holy Spirit is Creator, he is at the same time the Spirit of

Jesus Christ, but in such a way that the Father, the Son and the Holy Spirit are one God. And in the light of the First Reading we may add: the Holy Spirit gives life to the Church. She is not born from the human will, from man's reflection, from his ability or from his organizational capacity, if this were so she would have ceased to exist long ago, as happens with all that is human. Instead the Church is the body of Christ, enlivened by the Holy Spirit. The images of wind and fire, used by St Luke to portray the coming of the Holy Spirit (cf. *Acts* 2:2-3), evoke Sinai, where God revealed himself to the People of Israel and granted it his Covenant. "Mount Sinai was wrapped in smoke", we read in the Book of Exodus, "because the Lord descended upon it in fire" (19:18). Indeed Israel celebrated the 50th day after the Passover, after the commemoration of the flight from Egypt, as the feast of Sinai, the feast of the Covenant. When St Luke speaks of tongues of fire to represent the Holy Spirit, this Old Covenant is called to mind, established on the basis of the Law received by Israel on Sinai. Thus the event of Pentecost is represented as a new Sinai, as the gift of a new Covenant in which the Covenant with Israel was extended to all the peoples of the earth, in which all the barriers fall from the old Law and its heart appears holier and more unchangeable; in other words as love, which the Holy Spirit himself communicates and spreads, a love that embraces all things.

The extension of the Covenant to all the peoples
of the earth

At the same time the Law is expanded, it is opened, even though it becomes simpler: it is the New Covenant which the Spirit "writes" in the hearts of all who believe in Christ. The extension of the Covenant to all the peoples of the earth is represented by St Luke with a list of peoples, that is considerably long for that epoch (cf. *Acts* 2:9-11). With this we are told something most important: that the Church was catholic from the very outset, that her universality is not the result of the successive inclusion of various communities. Indeed, from the first moment the Holy Spirit created her as the Church of all peoples; she embraces the whole world, surmounts all distinctions of race, class and nation; tears down all barriers and brings people together in the profession of the triune God. Since the beginning the Church has been one, catholic and apostolic: this is her true nature and must be recognized as such. She is not holy because of her members' ability but because God himself, with his Spirit, never ceases to create her, purify her and sanctify her.

The most beautiful gift of his joy

Lastly, today's Gospel presents these beautiful words to us: "the disciples were glad when they saw the Lord" (*Jn* 20:20). These words are profoundly human. The Friend lost is present once again and those who were formerly distraught rejoice. But it says far more. For the lost Friend did not come from just anywhere but from the night of death; and he passed through it! He is not just anyone; indeed he is the Friend and at the same time the One who is the Truth that gives life to men and women; and what he gives is not just any kind of joy but joy itself, a gift of the Holy Spirit. Yes, it is beautiful to live because I am loved and it is the Truth who loves me. The disciples were glad when they saw the Lord. Today, at Pentecost, these words are also addressed to us, because in faith we can see him. In faith he comes among us and to us too he shows his hands and his side and we are glad. Therefore let us pray: Lord, show yourself! Make us the gift of your presence and we shall have the most beautiful gift: your joy.

Sources

Rediscovering Our Baptism: Message of his Holiness Benedict XVI for Lent 2011 from the Vatican, 4 November, 2010.

Strengthen our desire to change – Ash Wednesday: General Audience, Paul VI Audience Hall, Ash Wednesday, 9 March 2011.

Authentic conversion to God: Statio and penitential procession from the Church of St Anselm to the Basilica of St Sabina on the Aventine Hill, Holy Mass, blessing and imposition of the ashes, homily of His Holiness Benedict XVI, Basilica of St Sabina, Ash Wednesday, 9 March 2011.

Walking in Lent: Angelus, St Peter's square, First Sunday of Lent, 13 March 2011; Second Sunday of Lent, 20 March 2011; Third Sunday of Lent, 27 March 2011; Fourth Sunday of Lent, 3 April 2011; Fifth Sunday of Lent, 10 April 2011.

Road that leads to the living God – Palm Sunday: Celebration of Palm Sunday of the Passion of Our Lord, homily of His Holiness Benedict XVI, Saint Peter's Square, 26th World Youth Day, Sunday, 17 April 2011.

He makes us all one – the Lord's Supper: Mass of The Lord's Supper, homily of His Holiness Benedict XVI, Basilica of St John Lateran, Holy Thursday, 21 April 2011.

Way of the Cross – Good Friday: Way of the Cross at the Colosseum, address of His Holiness Benedict XVI, Good Friday, 22 April 2011.

Reason and freedom in creation – Easter Vigil: Easter Vigil, homily of His Holiness Benedict XVI, Saint Peter's Basilica, Holy Saturday, 23 April 2011.

Continuous resurrection within us – Octave of Easter: General Audience, St Peter's Square, Octave of Easter, Wednesday, 27 April 2011.

The gift of joy itself – Pentecost: Eucharistic Celebration on the Solemnity of Pentecost, homily of His Holiness Benedict XVI, Vatican Basilica, Sunday, 12 June 2011.

Lent & Easter
Catholic Customs & Traditions

Spanning the seasons of Lent, Easter and to Pentecost, this booklet describes the rich heritage of customs and traditions long practiced by Catholics down the ages, up to today. Shrovetide, ashes, pancakes, Mardi Gras, fasting, almsgiving, pilgrimage, special saints' days, simnel cake, palms, Easter eggs, Easter bunnies, Holy week, hot cross buns, processions - these are just some of the many fascinating traditional practices associated with the religious festivals. The liturgy in turn enriches their meaning, as we rediscover how faith and everyday life are mutually supportive and instructive.

Joanna Bogle is an author, broadcaster, and journalist whose books include several historical biographies and *A Yearbook of Seasons and Celebrations* with ideas on how to celebrate all the seasons of the Church's year.

ISBN: 978 1 86082 630 6

CTS Code: D720

A world of Catholic reading at your fingertips...

Catholic Faith, Life & Truth for all

www.cts-online.org.uk

ctscatholiccompass.org

twitter: @CTSpublishers

facebook.com/CTSpublishers

Catholic Truth Society, Publishers to the Holy See.